Passionate Curiosity

I have no special talents
I am only
Passionately Curious.
— Albert Einstein

Library of Congress Control Number: 2014918187

ISBN: 978-0-578-15288-2

Copyright © 2014
By Ram S. Arora.

All rights reserved. No part of this book shall be reproduced, stored in a retrieval system, photocopied, audio recorded, or transmitted by any other means, without written permission of the copyright-holder.
Publisher: Ram S. Arora

For bulk purchases:
Tel: 248-202-0000
E-mail: holiramg@gmail.com

Contents

Prelude	7
Artistry and Curiosity	11
Anxiety and Curiosity	15
Boredom and Curiosity	23
Creativity and Curiosity	33
Futurology and Curiosity	43
God and Curiosity	53
Lifeology and Curiosity	61
Mathology and Curiosity	69
Prosperity and Curiosity	81
Tranquility and Curiosity	89
Simplicity and Curiosity	97
Postlude	107

Curiosity Begets
Creativity, Knowledge, Prosperity, Simplicity, Tranquility, Scientists, Freedom
Incuriosity Breeds
Lethargy, Ignorance, Poverty, Complexity, Boredom, Politicians, Dependency,

Curiosity Prelude

The BEST investment
Any nation can craft
To prosper curiosity and prosperity
To engage the finest curious minds
To discover the laws of nature
Is that scientific education be
Totally TUITION-FREE and
Science and Math Instructors
Be remunerated
Better than all other
Professionals.

Prelude

It is a miracle that curiosity survives formal education.
— Albert Einstein

The words *why* and *how* are only about a millennium old. Subsequent to *why* and *how*, the words *where, when, which, who, what, whom* and *if* were conceived. The word *curiosity* that comprises all queries is about half a millennium old. Curiosity now covers many behavioral aspects, e.g.: intense desire to know, meddling, eagerness, inquisitiveness, interestingness, thirst for knowledge intrusiveness, investigation, mental acquisitiveness, and questioning, etc. The seed of life - the DNA molecule - has the curiosity gene programmed into it.

Over three thousand years, three passionately curious geniuses, Newton, Maxwell and Einstein, broke into the most fascinating mysteries of the universe. Many hundreds of curious geniuses followed these three and discovered many more laws of nature. Their discoveries brewed millions of inventions, that made the journey of our lives super-fast, comfortable, joyful, mechanized and lazy, free and enslaved, busy and lonely, etc.

Newton's curiosity marveled at the earth and all the planets going around the sun, moon around the earth, every object falling back when hurled up, forces accelerating material bodies and lots more. He developed mathematical tools to express the laws of mechanics very concisely and precisely. Thousands of curious minds used Newton's discoveries and mathematics to break into more mysteries of nature. Maxwell, a genius and mathematician of the highest order, divulged all the secrets of complete spectrum of the omnipresent electromagnetic fields expressed in four vector calculus equations. Maxwell's equations are as potent as Einstein's prophetic energy to mass conversion equation. His mathematical formulations showed that light was only a part of the very big spectrum of electromagnetic waves. Speed of light calculated from his equations was found to be correct. He was inventor of color photography, discoverer of the true nature of Saturn rings and remarkable contributor to thermodynamics.

Einstein, the greatest scientist of our times, believed that "The most incomprehensible thing about the universe is that it is comprehensible". He truly comprehended and could explain mysteries of nature better than anyone else. His energy to mass equivalence equation $E = mc^2$ was the foundation of nuclear fission and fusion of elements to produce immense amount of energy.

Newton's sincere conviction that "I do not know what I may appear to the world; but to myself I seem to have been only like a boy playing on the seashore, and diverting myself in now and then finding a smoother pebble or a prettier shell than ordinary, whilst the great ocean of truth lay all undiscovered before me." bolsters the truth that all the unearthed mysteries of nature are infinitely huge compared to all the discoveries made so far. It would be interesting now to explore the personality and temperament of curiosity and creativity.

Artistry and Curiosity

*All that
Eyes desire to see,
Ears want to hear,
Tongues like to taste,
Bodies crave to walk on,
Minds feel tranquil about,
Calls for
Curious artists' creative Imaginations.
Monotonous moments of life
Are alleviated by
Artistic creators of
Cartoons, delicatessens, fiction,
Humor, jewelry, landscapes, Magics,
Music, paintings, poems,
Sculptures, shopping malls,
Songs, symphonies,
Vacation Resorts
And
Wardrobes.*

Artistry and Curiosity

- Newton's laws of gravitational forces and Einstein's energy to mass equation $E=mc^2$ sprouted from the highest degree of curiosity. The expedition to the moon materialized due to the power of curiosity of thousands of scientists and mathematicians.
- Curiosity mothered all mathematics, cell-phones, global positioning system , worldwide permeating internet structure, technically based medical diagnostics, steam, gasoline, jet engines, hydrogen-powered rockets, half a mile tall buildings, potent computing hardware and software languages, all wireless gadgets, programmable robots, flying machines and information technology.
- Only a small fraction of population enjoys a life ingrained in curiosity. Rest of the humanity suffers from anxiety; a little anxiety that keeps men waiting for a better tomorrow; a lot of anxiety that needs dangerous drugs to bury it temporarily.
- All autocrats and bureaucrats are biological robots. Any concept of curiosity cannot and does not exist in their vocabulary. They are victims of anxiety all their lives.
- Most of schooling stuffs young minds with cooked recipes to make a living and to suffer from a totally unadventurous, monotonous life that lacks the ingredient called curiosity. Autocratic schooling is planned and executed to convert

Artistry and Curiosity

curious young minds into obedient robots.

- ❖ Let us not permit schools ram down our kids' throats tailored information and pollute their natural instinct of curiosity. Any education that does not nurture curiosity is emotionally regressive.
- ❖ Every infant is the true embodiment of curiosity. Well planned upbringing smothers it. The characteristic called curiosity is the most important property the mind learns by. Without curiosity intelligence is blank.
- ❖ A curiosity-pill will be the supreme invention. Curiosity has sprouted all prosperity, It is the dynamics of life. It is programmed in the DNA molecule.
- ❖ Happiness shrivels without a curious mind; for curiosity is the source of happiness and it is the only anti-dote of boredom.
- ❖ Why, how, where, when, if and then are the foundation stones of curiosity. It is unassailable nature of Nature. And it is what separates man from monkey.
- ❖ The realm of curiosity begins at the very subatomic particles and goes beyond the vast galaxies. No mystery of Nature can hide from the power of curiosity.
- ❖ Curiosity is intelligence submerged in exuberance. Science is about discovering the mysteries of nature. Curiosity is synonym of science.

Anxiety and Curiosity

*"I am a very old man
and have suffered a great
many misfortunes, most of
which never happened."*
--Mark Twain

Anxiety and Curiosity

*Anxiety swaps real happiness
of today with imaginary worry
of tomorrow.*

Anxiety and curiosity are two opposite ends of the long pole on which life lingers. We arrive into this world as a bundle of curiosity; as we grow, age and wither, curiosity shrinks, anxiety expands and mind is always occupied with a mixture of these two sensations in varying proportions. Sadly, as the doors of life are about to close, and time arrives for us to return to wherever we came from, we really go back as a bundle of anxiety.

Mind is never at rest. It is wondering and wandering every moment of its existence. Even when all organs of the body are asleep, the mind is amazingly running around all kinds of totally unreal scenes, people and provisions. Of over 250 emotional states of mind, anxiety and curiosity are very important components of the list of emotions. Curiosity is relatively much easier to figure out than anxiety.

Both anxiety and curiosity are about the times that have yet to arrive from tomorrow, next year or many years hence. Man is either curious or anxious about what is to come. Whilst being curious is not worrisome, being anxious is. The desire to overcome ignorance calls for curiosity. An anxious mind is not looking for any knowledge, it just awaits the next moment of life with some kind of imaginary worry.

Anxiety and Curiosity

When we leave the warmth and comfort of our mothers' womb, we scream as if we are very unhappy. To begin with we are totally helpless, vulnerable and blank-brained. Newborn of no other species is so defenseless as human infants. To survive all we knew was how of suckle from a nipple. For many years we had to be fed, cleaned, bathed, clothed, and taught one word at a time. All our senses, hearing, visual, taste, smell and touch begin feeding our blank brains very fast. As we grow up, we are curious about every tangible and intangible piece of environment. We do not suffer from any anxiety of any kind; we are unaware of any emotion termed anxiety.

Then we continue to grow up. Our mind starts building a frame that increases in rigidity as time goes by. Sooner than later, by the time we enter into our teens, this frame takes the final form, and the foundation of our life is pretty well set. What we hear, taste, see, or we are made to see, taught or not taught, given to or taken from, how we are hated or loved, the way we are spoken to, the way our words are rejected or accepted, how we are permitted to exhibit ourselves in speech or person to our parents, friends, teachers and relatives determine what we would like, hate, fear, love, desire, hope for, accept, or reject all through the rest of our life unless we are fortunate enough to stray into a great deal of such knowledge that will open the knots of our aged mental frame and replace them with new ones. This change can come if we can muster a lot of discipline and determination and we are willing to take a lot of risk - a hard but possible task.

When very young we were not shy to look and stare at any stranger; we were not afraid of placing our finger on a burning candle; we would jump into a swimming pool without any fear of drowning; a snake would not scare us; we could sing and dance before a big audience; we would ask any question without any feeling of ignorance. Our whole being was anxiety-less.

Anxiety epidemiology of the whole world is an interesting and bewildering set of facts. Though the United States is one of the most prosperous country, it has the highest prevalence of anxiety disorder. Whilst global average is only 4.5%, the United States average is 29%. It may not be erroneous to analyze and conclude that the American politicians have mutilated and destroyed long lived very happy family structure; they have shattered closely held lives for heinous prolonging their power-grab of their thrones. Man suffers from stressful anxiety or enjoys simple peaceful curiosity on all simple elements of his life from the very beginning to the very end of his life.

It should not be difficult to accept the fact that all positive emotions like acceptance, affection, compassion, empathy, ecstasy, euphoria, gratitude, forgiveness, hope, interest, love, pleasure, pride and sympathy are not related to anxiety, or any other stressful state of mind. And also, all negative emotions like aggression, apathy, boredom, contempt, depression, envy, frustration, grief, guilt, hatred, hostility, hysteria, loneliness, paranoia, pity, and rage are root causes of stressful state of mind, that may be termed as an anxious mind.

Anxiety starts building up due to all kinds of normal and abnormal events that are common to all of us as we grow. Until we are not burdened with to earn our own livelihood, look after own needs and wants, and solve our own personal problems, anxiety does not occupy much of our minds. But in this period too, childhood friendship, school performance, relationship with parents and siblings can be a serious root of anxiety. When we begin to stand on our own feet to face all the simple and complex challenges of survival, we have to deal with our own personality, job performance and a boss along with a degree of curiosity and anxiety. If we decide to enjoy freedom and start our own business, we soon face a host of issues with much higher degree of curiosity and anxiety.

As we wither or bloom growing past our adulthood, we start becoming a compound mixture of a lot of happiness or grief, ethereal pain or pleasure, friendship or loneliness, prosperity or poverty, health or disease, simple or complex habits. Anxiety appears to be a very simple part of an ordinary and simple lifestyle, and a very complicated ingredient of any complex lifestyle. Anxiety hovers around us, *when*, a cop stops us for a traffic violation, we are running late for any important meeting, one of our loved ones is injured or is seriously sick, as jobless we go for a job-interview, our job-performance review is near, walking around a crime-infested neighborhood, a call from a doctor about the result of our biopsy is close, a baby is on her way into this world, any problematical surgical procedure begins, a judge is about to rule on a criminal proceeding, and the near or far off future is truly or mistakenly not in our favor.

Separation Anxiety Disorder is now a very usual and frightful component of American culture. The building blocks of a happy life that ooze out of human-bonds built into a structure called "family" are weakening, disintegrating and vanishing. For the ill democratic-autocracy *Divide and Rule* weapon is omnipotent; the ruling elite, that suffers from many mental disorders of its own is continually busy inventing more grounds as to how the ruled could and should sue each other more often. All lawsuits keep the litigants anxious and lawyers' oligarchy curious all through long and rewarding court-combats.

Psychotherapist have another anxiety card in their pocket; they call it situational anxiety. Standing and waiting in a long line for any service is not enjoyable to anyone; being in a crowded elevator, movie hall, or having to sit in between two very obese or smelly passengers in a plane, bus or anywhere is a source of serious anxiety. Anxiety is a silent component of all troublesome emotions and curiosity is a vibrant element of all joyful emotions. Curiosity makes life rich without any riches; it keeps life positive, open and interesting. Curiosity is the only spice that can replace all psychiatric drugs and psychotherapy that keep anxiety buried under the skull.

Many drugs induce and may augment anxiety. A few of those drugs are: blood pressure drugs, oral contraceptives, amphetamines, thyroid medicines, and a number of antidepressants. All nomenclatures used by the medical and drug communes for ailments and drugs are to sophisticate their occupations for bigger pecuniary gains. For anti-panic and anti-anxiety drugs they invented the term *anxiolytics*. Nearly all classes of intoxications including the one caused by alcohol hide or trim down anxiety. A class of drugs labeled Benzodiazepines are recommended for the treatment of various degrees of anxiety; however, these drugs in the long run may cause depression, ,dizziness, insomnia, headache, unsteadiness and sedation. Benzodiazepines are seriously addictive chemicals and trigger over half a million

Anxiety and Curiosity

emergency visits to hospitals a year. Psychiatric medical commune has labeled all supposedly nonstandard, deviant or unusual behaviors as disorders and not as diseases. Peculiarly this commune does not want to or is seriously incompetent to come up with any objective measure of any of the hundreds of disorders they have invented and labelled; the commune is proud of imposing their subjectively biased diagnosis to addict millions of lifestyle burdened brains with hazardous chemicals. They keep on attacking and interfering with these lifestyle disorders with slingshots of hardly a dozen commercially promoted substances and their derivatives. Drugs shrink curiosity and bury anxiety and slowly drain a lively human being of natural sense of peace and calmness.

Conclusively!
Anxiety and Curiosity

- ❖ Anxiety is like worrying about disasters in the immediate or distant future. Curiosity is analogous to expecting some positive and interesting outcome from any creative activity.
- ❖ Anxiety is a disabling stress. Curiosity is a wholesome state of mind.
- ❖ Ignorance propagates anxiety. Knowledge or quest for knowledge proliferates curiosity.
- ❖ A very large mass of humanity breathes off their lives in anxiety to acquire more earthly goods; a little humanity lives on enjoyable curiosity.
- ❖ Anxiety impedes happiness. Curiosity facilitates it.

Boredom and Curiosity

The two foes of human happiness are pain and boredom.... Life presents, in fact, a more or less violent oscillation between the two. Needy surroundings and poverty produce pain; while, if a man is more than well off, he is bored.
—*Arthur Schopenhauer*

Boredom is burden on the brain, pain burden on the body. Addiction to drugs and drinking is the fastest fix, for they bury boredom and pain fast but only briefly, only briefly.

Boredom and Curiosity

Cure for Monotony is curiosity, Cure for curiosity is more curiosity.
—*Albert Einstein*

Boredom manifests itself in a way of life that is drenched with incuriosity, detachment, dullness, indifference, lassitude and lethargy, and is a somber misery we all face in diverse degrees. Only human life-form has to struggle with boredom. Animals are fortunate and superior to man for they do not face this misfortune. The size of and suffering from boredom have seen no variation for millennia. Only the schemes and styles to run away from boredom keep on changing as the shapes of prosperity, poverty, technology, speed of life and godly faiths change.

Most men spend their lives off as biological robots. Their brains are too big for whatever they do or have to do from birth to death. Consequently they suffer from very high degree of boredom and look for various channels to kill their disposable time. This is the class of men that has been destructive all through the history. When life becomes lusterless, threatening, lonely, loveless or sickening, monotony invades; life is then empty and depressing. Life cannot put up with emptiness. Nature abhors vacuum as much in inert space as in a living mind. So a monotonous living mind ends up with all kinds of dangerous debris.

Boredom and Curiosity

Like innumerable states of mind, boredom too is objectively immeasurable and indefinable. Psychosomatically, boredom is about wanting a tangible or an intangible environment of which a bored person is not sure. Boredom may be a mixture of frustration, idleness, disgust, fatigue, indifference, apathy, incuriosity, dullness and all that makes one feel isolated from rest of the world. Boredom is not an emotion as some psychologists claim it to be. Boredom cannot be treated or cured through medical intervention or psychotherapy. Happiness to a very large degree is about defending against boredom that can be achieved very inexpensively or very extravagantly. Also, happiness is more about inner wealth than outer tangible possessions. Only a very small fraction of man's brain power has accomplished all the technological wonders and economic prosperity that all the humanity is enjoying today. More than 90% of all the humans who visited this planet depleted their lives as beasts of burden. The yoke, saddle and pay-load are the elements a beast of burden has to put up with every moment of his long or short monotonous life.

Whilst the poor all their lives tussle to satisfy their needs, the rich employ their riches to defend against boredom. Colossal enterprises become colossal simply on the expertise to keep boredom of the rich in check. The rich profess that charm of natural beauty is more captivating two thousand miles away, or the skill to smack a tiny white ball from one hole to the next is worth learning and very entertaining. The lifestyle of the masses, devoid of any element of curiosity, is replete with paltry pastimes. A incurious, feeble and drained mind needs to escape from very ordinary obstacles of life with drugs and alcohol. Vulgarity is a common denominator of this class that is aggressive, anxious, depressed, rebellious, and thrill seeker.

Though a virtuous mind is too wonderful for words, it saves the body it resides in from many hardships, disasters and destructive effects of boredom. The tragedy associated with most skills for making a living is the boredom and sickening stress that descends on our lives due to repetitive and non-challenging nature of the responsibilities we have to carry out. As time goes by, even the work that we loved to begin with and clamored for smolders our hearts and minds. This is the reason why the quitting time of every day and weekends, holidays, and vacations are anxiously waited for. Most who work for others, if given choice between going and not going to work and still getting paid, will choose abstaining. They want to have fun, take it easy, and live a life drinking and loafing around.

The task of making a living, the task that is lifelong for most, if not enjoyable, is burdensome and may cause many health problems. For those who work for themselves, even repetitive dull work is not so dull, because they receive superior return of their hard work. Livelihood must be a joy for the life to be enjoyable. No life could be superior to the one that is in love with the process of earning a living. Bored to Death is a very common exclamation we hear. Boredom, monotony or ennui may be the root of many dangerous problems, particularly drugs and crimes that we face. For most boredom comes in short spurts, for some it is a long lasting stress. Drinking, drugs and gambling are universal defenseless weapons to ward off boredom.

Nature Deficiency Disorder is now a believable mental disorder that buries the brain in boredom. The rich and the poor engulfed in and on the streets, roads, malls, restaurants, entertainment-centers, offices and factories of megalopolis suffer from Nature Deficiency Disorders. All edifices created by man, skyscrapers, museums, fountains, mega malls, vacation resorts, gambling-casinos become unexciting very fast. No natural scenery ever becomes monotonous. The music of ocean-waves is refreshing no matter how many years we live by it. Listening to same man-made music very soon becomes wearisome. Every natural phenomenon is thrilling. No rainbow, fall, running water stream, full moon, sunrise, sunset, can ever be dreary. No instruction or lesson is needed to enjoy nature. All animals roaming around with freedom in a forest look more interesting than all those imprisoned in a zoo. One does not need any kind of concentration to enjoy nature to ward off melancholy.

Being suicidal over constantly being bored is a well established fact. There have been many notable people that committed suicide simply because they could not find life interesting and worth living. These suicidal personalities included famous politicians, fiction-writers, lawyers, singers, song-writers, wrestlers, embezzlers, criminals, players and actors; none of them were scientific, technical or mathematical people for the simple reason that a mind engaged with curiosity in their professions did not face any lackluster environment. Anxiety and depression are significantly related to dullness. Bottomless boredom needs to be buried in drunkenness and it is so buried as a rule or as a way out.

The United States of American with only 5% of the world population confines 25% of all prisoners of the world. Nearly 50 million seriously addictive Americans spend over $100 billion dollars on cocaine, heroin, pot and meth every year. The fundamental root of the above pathetic facts is world-weariness, collapse of from way back creative and curious lifestyles.

All the techniques to defend against boredom are very simple and free if one does not believe that good times and fun are accessible at least a thousand miles away from where one lives, or without intoxication no relaxation is possible, or creative mental and physical activities are tedious, or holding on to one's own money unwaveringly is the only way get rich, or an organized way of living is pathetic, or the boss at work has no ability to be a boss, or eating out is more enjoyable than preparing one's own food, or inactively glued to watching sports is really a great fun. Most importantly when inactivity takes hold of one's soul, boredom is in control.

Why do so many diligent and intelligent students anxiously await weekends to run into their sororities and fraternities for drinking binges? Is the kind of knowledge they are trying to accumulate so boring that a safety valve has to kick off to release all the accumulated monotony during the week days? Drinking has not proved to trim down any misery including boredom; beyond a shadow of a doubt it buries melancholy in an intoxicated mind. What does drinking accomplish? Neuroscience discovers that it disconnects us from our minds; whatever it means, alcohol molecules erect many barriers among various modules of physical brain. Very briefly, drinking then means that it is for one to escape from oneself. Does it translates then as escaping from boredom?

Over 18% medical students spree-drink during schooling and internships. Why is medical commune too not immune from monotony, and why does it suffer from drugs and alcohol abuse more than many other communes. Most medical practitioners have to do repetitive, though very remunerative, monotonous jobs, without adding any new knowledge to their specialties all their lives. The latest drug use data from the U.S. Substance Abuse and Mental Health Services Administration, indicated that an average of 130,000 doctors, nurses, medical technicians and health care aides a year were abusing or dependent on illicit drugs. Various studies suggest the number could be far higher; an estimated one in 15 practitioners will fall into drug or alcohol abuse at some point in their lives, mirroring the general population. Weirdly only a small fraction of medical commune is curious to enhance its expertise. Why it professes that a regular ingestion of alcohol is good for the heart, knowing well that every molecule of alcohol attacks the liver and the brain immediately; the answer is that alcohol temporarily buries boredom from which medicos go through no less than the patients they try to cure or treat.

A Boozer's Monologue
Thank You, God!

I had babyhood packed of pleasure
But as I grew into adolescence in leisure
The sparkles of life started to departure
Then as years went by my enthusiasm
I was assaulted by strange destitution
My soul immersed in a bizarre pollution
Friends I had many, but I don't fathom
What they were, or what I was to them
You granted me all the ingredients
To kill boredom by many means
Sunrise, sunset, sunshine, rainbows
Flowers, canyons and mountain-peaks
Colorful birds singing their songs
If friends can treat or cure monotony
Then you don't need gin or whiskey
When a sip of scotch slips down my esophagus

Boredom and Curiosity

A million blissful slivers go up my spinal column
Boozed up, I don't feel disoriented
They claim, boozing is dreadful and wicked
But I claim this remedy dances in my mind

Conclusively!
Boredom and Curiosity

- ❖ The only Cure for boredom is curiosity.
- ❖ Curiosity and boredom are two opposite extremities of life.
- ❖ Only human life-form suffers from boredom.
- ❖ At least half the crimes are committed to defend against boredom, the root of many evils, crimes and drug abuse.
- ❖ History is mostly about how boredom had to be fought off through deadly-rampages.

Creativity and Curiosity

If a man's most ingenious and potent computer could ever discover and then mathematically so concisely formulate what Newton, Maxwell and Einstein did, we then could and should equate the man to a human-God.

Creativity and Curiosity

Creativity is intelligence having fun.
—Albert Einstein

Einstein's belief that "The most incomprehensible thing about the universe is comprehensible" did not mean that "The most comprehensible thing about the mind — the very mind that Einstein applied to discover many mysteries of the universe — is that the mind is incomprehensible." Mind without a doubt is the most mysterious puzzle in the universe. Brain — the anatomical hardware, wherein the mind resides — has been hypothesized to have more than 100 million gigabytes of memory; the memory that perhaps is structured by electronic states of individual atoms of the brain-neurons. The brain perhaps functions as a bio-atomic computer. How does the most powerful computer compare with a mind!

If a man's most ingenious and potent computer could ever discover and then mathematically so concisely formulate what Newton, Maxwell and Einstein did, we then could and should equate the man to a human-God. All tangible and intangible resources, like imagination, ingenuity, inspiration, resourcefulness, vision, originality, inventiveness and wealth that keep us comfortable, joyful, healthy, safe, peaceful, free and educated are children of creativity. Passionate curiosity of scientists discovers the laws and mysteries of nature, and these laws are foundations of great inventions.

It is interesting to examine how humans transport, convey, live, make or fail their lives to create, consume and destroy wealth. The techniques, manners and styles of livelihoods have been in continual transition from the very beginning of the history. All creative or destructive livelihoods, in order of significance, are dependent on:

- Theoretical knowledge and physical skills
- Motivation and drive
- Cultural and social constraints
- Political regulations and freedom
- Natural resources
- Production technology
- Financial and mental capital
- Information technology
- Transportation of resources
- Supply, demand and marketing skills

From the best to the worst in terms of achievements, impact on humanity, peace, love and comfort, men may be classified as follows:

- *Discoverers and inventors, academic theorists:* They are the scientists in top academic schools and research institutes that expand the work of geniuses in many directions. Money and fame is of little temptation to them. Their dedication to expand the frontiers of knowledge creates all the progress, comforts and also terrible misuse of new knowledge.

- *Wealth creators:* They apply proven technology and information to generate wealth and employment of an amazing order.
- *Entertainers, poets, musicians, playwrights:* They portray and play life's joys, tragedies, emotions, laughter, good and bad times to let days and years roll by softly. Without them we will perish of boredom.
- *God's messengers:* They invent all kinds of Gods and Goddesses to direct and send their followers to hell or heaven. To be taken genuinely they have to look serious all their lives.
- *Human-robots, slaves and serva*nts: Almost 95% population falls in this category. They love to take orders and hate to think for themselves. Academic degrees do not free them from this slavery. Like mechanized components of a machine, their brains get programmed to do only very few tasks all their lives.
- *Morons*: Criminals, alcoholics, drug addicts and public (government) employees. Their minds suffer from petrifaction due to very little use of their brain-cells.
- *Monarchs and politicians:* They stand at the

lowest rung of human ladder. Their main objective is to rob and curb human-freedom. Freedom is an unintelligible concept to them.

It is very interesting to observe that **ten greatest scientists:** Einstein, Newton, Galilei , Curie, Archimedes, Born, Tesla, Maxwell, Kepler, da Vinci; **ten greatest inventors:** Edison, Wright Brothers, Franklin, Babbage, Watt, Bell, Berners Lee, Archimedes, Galilei, da Vinci; and **ten greatest mathematicians:** Newton, Gauss, Euler, Riemann, Poincare, Lagrange, Leibnitz, Fermat, Hilbert, Euclid, all were born in the same very small region of the world. During the last one hundred years people of Jewish descent grabbed 20% of Nobel Prizes in medicine, chemistry and physics, despite the fact that Jews make less than 1% population of the world.

We are born in an ocean of very powerful social, religious, cultural, racial, and political currents and depths. Rarely could one stand outside these currents and feel how the forces of these currents sway big masses of people into all kinds of constructive or destructive directions. We read, study, and assimilate history, human nature, philosophy, sociology, and a host of many related facts and still keep going through many cycles of rise and fall. As long as Providence does not decide to change human nature, we are destined to repeat the same fate many million times over. We may claim that man is the finest, most gifted,

Creativity and Curiosity

and intelligent creature of nature, but he is also the only cursed one, for he is the only one that must collect and hoard more than is needed, eat more than the body is willing to accept, and, worst of all, enslave and kill his own kind for fun and no good reason. And his will to conquer and rule his fellow beings comes alive at birth and dies with his death. "Knowledge is power" is not exactly true. How we use knowledge is what really matters. Minds rusting in ponds of knowledge are omnipresent.

Most of us are so deeply tranced, hypnotized, programmed, and brainwashed by all the audio and visual information that has been absorbed by our minds, both voluntarily and involuntarily, during our lives that we have absolutely no inkling that our thoughts, reasoning, beliefs, faith, and plans really grew in a murky pond. We are immersed in this pond, in a way similar to being immersed in the atmosphere of air; and therefore we have no real perception of our mental frames. We are like a frog in a well, just as a well is a frog's world, our pond of ignorance and knowledge is our world. What we don't know is millions of order of magnitude more than what we know. The most unfortunate and tragic truth is that we will not in the course of our lifetimes discover any benevolent and clear minded soul that will be able and willing to pull us out of the trance we are in. Only a very tiny fraction of us will ever realize and wake up and discover them and try to learn what should be learnt.

Creativity and Curiosity

Following are only few of the thousands of devices, machines and materials, scores of creative, curious, scientific and mathematical minds discovered, invented and mass produced over the last many centuries.

Adding machine, addressograph, airplane, airship, antiseptic, arc lamp, aspirin, atom bomb, automobile, bakelite, balloon, ballpoint pen, barbed wire, bicycle tires bifocal lens, bullet, bunsen burner, burglar alarm, cannon carburetor, carpet sweeper, car radio, cash register, cellophane, celluloid, cement, chain drive, chlorine, chronometer, cinema, clock, dacron, dental plate, diesel engine, disc brake, electric battery, electric blanket, electric fan, electric generation, electric lamp, DC electric motor, AC electric motor, electromagnetic induction, electronic computer, elevator, musical film, fluorine, food frozen, fountain pen, gas lighting, generator, stained glass, glider, gramophone, gyro-compass, helicopter, hovercraft, helium, iron working, jet engine, laser, lathe, launderette, laws of gravitation and motion, lightning conductor, locomotive, loudspeaker, machine gun, margarine, safety match , microphone, electron microscope , motorcycle, motor scooter, neon lamp, cosmopolitan theatre, night club, nineteenth laws of planetary motion, nylon, oxygen, ozone, paper, parachute, parchment, parking meter, phonograph, photography, piano, porcelain, potter's wheel, pneumatic tire, printing press, rotary printing, propeller ship, proton, pyramid, radar, radioactivity, radio telegraphy, rayon, safety razor, electric razor, reaper, record, refrigerator, revolver, rocket engine, waterproof rubber, vulcanized rubber, rubber tires, safety pin, sewing machine, sea-going ship, silicones, silk manufacture, skyscraper, slide rule, eyeglasses, spinning frame, steam engine, steel production, stainless steel stethoscope, electric streetcar, submarine, synthesizer, military tank, telegraph, telegraph codes, telephone, telescope, time recorder, tractor, transformer, transistor, typewriter, uranium, vaccination, electric washing machine, self-winding watch, wheel, windmill, writing, xerography, x-ray, zero, and zip fastener.

Historically, with rare exceptions, all outstanding inventions, great discoveries, and most rewarding business ideas came from the minds and muscles of men and women of ordinary means. So, a wealthy birth is a poor ground for ambition to survive, but poverty is a better ground, but not a sure bet, for an aspiration to grow. Dissatisfaction, disappointment and frustration may strengthen our drive for accomplishment. We can train our minds to stay curious and be more interested in the natural world around us. Only an inquiring and learning mind can continue to be a healthy and content mind.

Conclusively! Creativity and Curiosity

- ❖ Creative visionaries assemble expertise of many disciplines to allocate expensive resources to plan and manage gigantic enterprises.
- ❖ Creativity is not possible without curiosity. One of the many aspects of creativity is to translate complexity into simplicity.
- ❖ Originality, imagination, inspiration, ingenuity, vision and resourcefulness are seeds of creativity.
- ❖ Creativity alters boredom into excitement, knowledge into entertainment, money into jobs, war into peace, and lethargy into activity.
- ❖ There is unlimited scope for creativity in every art, gadget, skill, design, landscape, magic, celebration, speech, humor and unfortunately in deceptive politics.

Futurology and Curiosity

Futurology and Curiosity

Arrogance and Ignorance

Of the infinite mysterious miracles of the universe, only few have been grasped, those too only fractionally. Can energy and matter exist independent of each other, how does energy glue itself to matter, does time flow if all matter is stationary, what is the physical nature of gravitational and electromagnetic fields, how does a DNA molecule build an extremely complex life-form so fast, what is an irrefutable definition of life? These are only few questions of millions and millions.

To predict future for sure, for fifty or hundred years hence, is only a display of both arrogance and ignorance of any predictor. The future may see compact and efficient personal flying machines, successful manipulations of DNA molecule to control many genetic ailments, versatile programmable robots for all repetitive tasks, very strong and light construction materials to erect ten miles tall structures, and many similar feats. Fathoming any inconceivable mysteries of the universe may modify the future inconceivably. Imagine if energy could be extracted safely via nuclear fission or fusion in a few cubic feet space, or a brains's memory could be transferred to some other brain, or ageing gene(s) could be halted, or the power of ruling elite could be neutered, or a man could magically turn other man to ashes, how will then future look like?

Futurology and Curiosity

I fear the day when technology overlaps our humanity. It will be then that the world will have permanent ensuing generations of idiots.
— *Albert Einstein*

Half a millennium ago, Leonardo da Vinci, a genius who was an anatomist, architect, botanist, cartographer, engineer, inventor, painter, geologist, mathematician, musician, sculptor, and writer was born in the antiquity of ignorance. He was blessed with voracious curiosity and immense inventive imagination. He was the best futurologist we know. He foresaw flying machines, solar cells, armored vehicles, adding machines, optical instruments, hydrodynamic devices and host of many other mechanisms that became a realty centuries after his predictions.

Futurists, futurologists, and futurology are all about how the tools of technology, and any new discoveries of the mysteries of nature may curiously and extraordinarily transform man's technological, autocratic and cultural future. The popular quote that "man is born free and everywhere he is in chains" is fundamentally false; the truth is that "man is born in chains and has to struggle hard all through his life to stay chain-free." In antiquity liberal education was about liberty, now it is only about how to perpetuate slavery, dependence and crime. Though all liberally educated and trained professionals boogie on the pillars of technology, they loathe technologists and technology. The tools of technology have effortlessly empowered the ruling autocratic bureaucracy and bureaucratic autocracy to enchain the ruled. Futurologists must foresee if future can make man free or freer.

Constituents of whole life may be segregated into health, food, learning, earning, communication, transport, entertainment, crime and dealing with autocratic regimes. Futurology is about what may be possible that could significantly alter the above constituents of life. Generating, storing, transmitting and cost of high density clean energy is at the forefront of what the future holds for the civilization. Personal compact, light, auto controlled and directed flying machines are feasible if cheap liquid hydrogen can be safely carried on board. Byways and highway due to very high cost of building and maintaining them should be a relic of antiquity.

Man made photoelectrosynthesis appears to have good promise to generate electric power in large quantity. Photosynthesis, the natural chemical reaction that all plant use to combine carbon dioxide, water and light to make carbohydrates and oxygen. Radiation from the sun to the planet earth is of the order of 175,000 Terawatts; only a fraction of this radiated energy from the sun is photosynthesized by the plants. Not only plants but algae and some bacteria also use photosynthesis to make carbohydrates. New scientific discoveries particularly in the field of capturing energy of the sun and very densely storing it inexpensively for inhabitation and transportation will alter our lifestyle most radically. Electrolysis of water by solar-cell electrical power can generate hydrogen in unlimited volumes. Hydrogen is the most abundant element in the universe and also on the earth; it does not exist on the earth in elemental form and has to be produced electrically or chemically. The energy density of highly compressed hydrogen is more than three times that of any other fuel including gasoline. Storing and safely carrying it on board is the puzzle that has to be cracked. Little flying machines to fly us around will be very feasible when we can safely sit on a tank of liquid hydrogen. How food is grown, without genetically altering it, increasing its per acre yield many folds, safely storing and distributing it to feed exponentially exploding human population is a crucial question futurologists encounter. To irrigate very efficiently with least amount of water, to save from pests without poisonous pesticides, to sow in wilderness without tilling, and to harvest robotically are some more tasks to be tackled.

> *If you think in terms of a year, plant a seed; if in terms of ten years, plant trees; if in terms of 100 years, teach the people.*
> — *Confucius*

Predictions about any future, whether about next 100 days or 100 years, cannot be given much credence. If suddenly a splendid genius like Newton, Maxwell or Einstein decides to visit the planet earth, unimaginable scientific and technological evolution and revolution may emerge. If suddenly any such wonders like cold fusion for energy, antigravity for flying around like birds, reprogramming of DNA molecules for modifying life-forms, storing energy very densely, instantaneously copying and transferring all the stored memory from one brain to another, was achievable, image of the future will be amazing and incredible However it is interesting to recognize what futurologists predict on the future of next 100 years:

- Extracting and using energy from the omnipresent electromagnetic and gravitational fields
- 3D constituted biomaterials and drugs
- 3D constituted fashion apparel
- 3D constituted membranes for healthy hearts
- 3D constituted human organs
- A biomedical chair for all noninvasive diagnostics
- A comprehensive vaccine for all infectious disease
- Accurate simulations of viruses
- Advanced nanotech clothing
- Alzheimer's disease curable
- An artificial intelligence brain
- Antarctica lush and blossoming
- Anti-aging intervention
- Aquaculture for world's seafood
- Assembling lines robots
- Auto natural fiction creation
- Auto programmed trading
- Battlefield robots
- Biochemical computers with holographic monitors and keyboards
- Biomedicines technology to slow down ageing
- Bionic eyes superior to human vision
- Biosynthesized uterus transplanted for pregnancy
- Biotech embedded sensors
- Brain implants to restore lost memories

Futurology and Curiosity

- Companionship robots
- Complete biosynthesized bladders
- Complex organ replacements grown from stem cells
- Computerized litigation articulation
- Conventional offices extinct
- Copying memory from one brain to another
- Dead people recreated holographically
- Depression and anxiety totally eliminated
- Digital robotic animals
- Domestic help robots
- Driverless personal vehicles
- Electromagnetic and electronic drugless anesthesia
- Electromagnetic pain interruption
- Exoskeletons for disabled people
- Extensive robotic surgery
- Fanatic faiths carry on murderous rampages.
- Full immersion virtual reality
- Full weather modeling
- Fully automated self-sufficient homes
- Fusion power widespread
- Fusion reactor
- Genetically engineered babies
- Heavy automation of supermarkets and retail environments
- Hepatitis C fully under control
- Hi-tech, highly automated intelligent buildings
- Holographic TV
- Holographic wall screens
- Home portable MRI diagnostics
- Human brain simulations
- Human-like AI widespread
- Hydrogen fuel cell vehicles
- Hypersonic airliners are entering service
- Implantable artificial kidney

Futurology and Curiosity

- Individual gene sequencing
- Individual tailored drugs
- Inexpensive sea-water desalination
- Institution of marriage almost dead
- In-vitro meats commercial
- Leukemia almost 100% curable
- Mega Geo engineering Projects
- Mind evaluation technology
- Miniature computers with big holographic monitors
- Mostly noninvasive diagnostics
- Music creation with robotic singing
- Nanobots for diagnostics and cures
- Nanofabricators commercially available
- Nanorobots in circulatory system
- Nanotech disposable clothes
- Nanotech self-assembling buildings
- Nanotechnology killing malignant cells without chemo or radiation therapies.
- Natural laws derivation from empirical data
- New biological limbs alternative to prosthesis
- Objective evaluation of eye field-vision-test
- Objective Eye glass prescription
- Objective mental disorders diagnostics
- Optogenetics reviving hippocampus memories
- Optogenetics: a neuromodulation technique
- Personal automated flying machines
- Policing robots
- Psychiatric objective evaluation,.
- Quantum computers abundantly commercial
- Recreational cyborgs
- Regenerated lost limbs for amputees
- Rejuvenation of aged heart muscle
- Repetitive manual work extinct
- Repetitive manufacturing jobs obsolete
- Reprogramming of DNA molecule

Futurology and Curiosity

- ❖ Resurrection of many extinct species
- ❖ Retailing service and cashier robots
- ❖ Robotic criminals
- ❖ Robotic hands matching human capabilities
- ❖ Robotic journalism
- ❖ Robotic movie actors
- ❖ Robotic subordinates
- ❖ Routine service robots, like airlines attendants
- ❖ Security robots, air travel, court attendance
- ❖ Skin optical devices for blood analysis
- ❖ Stem cell pharmacies
- ❖ Stem cell treatments to repair heart diseases
- ❖ Stress and anxiety disorders extinct
- ❖ Super jumbo jets like unique shopping centers
- ❖ Synthetic blood
- ❖ Synthetic brainpower
- ❖ Synthetic humans
- ❖ Synthetic proteins
- ❖ Teacher-less teaching
- ❖ Thought controlled digital devices
- ❖ Total noninvasive diagnostics
- ❖ Ultra High Definition flexible screen TV
- ❖ Very high yield household farms
- ❖ Virtual-digital brains
- ❖ War and defense services robots
- ❖ Wearable e-skins
- ❖ Wireless electric power transmission
- ❖ Word processing and texting by thinking

What knowledge is of most worth? The uniform reply is: Science. This is the verdict on all counts. For direct self-preservation, or the maintenance of life and health, the all-important knowledge is—science. For that indirect self-preservation which we call gaining a livelihood, the

knowledge of greatest value is—science. ...Alike for the most perfect production and present enjoyment of art in all its forms, the needful preparation is still—science. And for purposes of discipline—intellectual, moral, religious—the most efficient study is, once more—science.
—*Herbert Spencer*

Conclusively!
Futurology and Curiosity

- ❖ Curiosity is the most important element that holds the secrets of future.
- ❖ Any curious creative genius could prove all futurologists thoroughly erroneous and off the mark.
- ❖ Very high density, nontoxic, inexpensive and super-clean energy will jazz up the future more than any other invention or discovery will.
- ❖ Futurologists are the visionaries who have boundless capacity to imagine what may be possible.
- ❖ Superb natural curiosity brightens and lightens the future more than all other talents combined.

God and Curiosity

God and Curiosity

The word God is for me nothing more than the expression and product of human weaknesses, the Bible a collection of honorable, but still primitive legends which are nevertheless pretty childish. No interpretation no matter how subtle can change this.
—*Albert Einstein*

God and Curiosity

Coincidence is God's way of remaining anonymous.
—Albert Einstein

So blind is the curiosity by which mortals are possessed, that they often conduct their minds along unexplored routes, having no reason to hope for success, but merely being willing to risk the experiment of finding whether the truth they seek lies there.
—René Descartes

Man has been eternally curious of all the wonders he observes every moment of his life; so he invented, but could never discover the maker of all those wondrous mysteries. The curiosity to discover the whereabouts, profiles and plans of God or to explore His reasons to create this universe has never waned. On the contrary some faiths, particularly Hindus have invented more gods and goddesses than rest all the faiths combined; Hindus own gods for all worldly possession, needs and wants.

God has been like an eventual intoxicating drug for securing peace, or going for perpetual murderous rampage or spending whole life in a slothful slumber. No measure of curiosity, most truly an infinite amount of curiosity, may not make any dent in discovering an iota of whatever we call 'God'.

God and Curiosity

If death, disease, and all other natural calamities were not parts of life, God would have not been perhaps discovered or invented. For the real life, the way it presents itself, many painful events beyond the control of the living needed some imaginary entity to blame, held responsible, or appreciated. God, in fact a variety of Gods, have been given a variety of roles over the history of mankind. No segment of humanity, very ancient or modern, can be claimed to be superior or inferior to one over the other in regard to origins, kinds, forms, and functions of their God or Gods. All are equally ridiculous and or praiseworthy. If only we could comprehend this fact, immense amount of blood that has been shed and torture practiced by the people of one God against the people of some other God could have been prevented.

However, we have to emphasize that God and Gods are needed, they have important functions; the most important of all these functions is the one that keeps man's horrible nature under control for imaginary or real fear of hell after death. And the next important function is the consolation that we can receive from our God when we face a tragedy; this consolation is far superior to what psychotherapists and psychiatrist can provide us with after relieving our wallets of a lot of its contents.

Many great scientists and mathematicians, Newton, Faraday, Maxwell, Descartes, Einstein, Planck, Neumann, invoked God in face of the

God and Curiosity

incomprehensibility of the infinite universe and its mysteries around them.

The law of causality, that is, there has to be a cause to every effect; one thing has to happen for another thing to happen. This law appears to be irrefutable because no one has ever seen an exception to what it states. So, the atheists have a forceful argument that if we need a God to create the universe, we do need a second God to make the first God, and so on.

However, the gamble that the great mathematician and philosopher, Blasé Pascal, suggested is worth taking. He argued, believing in God could spring honesty, humility, generosity and truthfulness, whereas, atheism is the root cause of every poisonous mind. If one believes in God, and He did not exist, one has nothing to lose. On the other hand, if He did exist, and one who thought to the contrary, has only the hell to visit.

God is invoked when the body is withered, and is too weak to stand the rigors of daily life, and its systems fail to provide it with the needed nourishments, and it can no longer carry its own weight, and it does not find anything new and fresh around it, and its ears refuse to hear, eyes cannot see, skin does not feel hot or cold, and its own descendants no longer want it around because it becomes burdensome to them, and its own mind does not want to be contained in its own body, then it must be the time for it to go and go forever.

God and Curiosity

Some kind of God then accompanies the end of life.

If we would philosophize in earnest, and give ourselves to the search after all the truths we are capable of knowing, we must, in the first place, lay aside our prejudices..... We must, in the next place, make an orderly review of the notions we have in our minds, and hold as true all and only those which we will clearly and distinctly apprehend. In this way we will observe,... that there is a God upon whom we depend; and after considering his attributes we will be able to investigate the truth of all other things, since God is the cause of them. —René Descarte

We must praise the philosophers who invented the bright idea that life is made of an entity called soul. The soul is invisible, incorruptible and immortal, a tiny part of God Herself; it moves from one body to another, when the previous body cannot sustain it. The destiny of soul has been made a lot more complicated. It must free itself from the torture of changing its bodies; it is possible only if the human body it is in passes a sinless lifetime. This is also like an invention to control man's terrible acts. Finally, the concept of soul may be totally ridiculous, but any faith in it reduces the pain when death comes too early to those who must still live.

Why is it almost impossible for the living to accept the end of life to be imminent, not predictable or optional? It is because the molecular codes of life appear to be only programmed to reach an end but not to accept it. We are, therefore, willing to go through an immense amount of torture not to arrive at where we must whether we like it or not.

We would depend a little less on scientific knowledge when non-material questions have to be settled, if we only remember that science deals with only material entities using material intermediaries like instruments and recorders, and makes material conclusions for material applications. Mind, God, soul and consciousness do not appear to be material in essence and so scientific methods and procedures cannot help us comprehend these abstract concepts.

God came into being very mysteriously
There is no beginning or end to Her creativity
She is also beyond the law of causality
This is all that goes into eternity
After God came into existence
She conceived and created the universe
All the stars, planets, black holes and galaxies
Visible and invisible materials
Gravitation, light, electrons, neutrons and positrons
Rivers, stream, oceans and mountains
She paid particular attention to planet earth
No reason, why?

Conclusively!
God and Curiosity

- ❖ Notwithstanding how God is comprehended, God is beyond curiosity, for God cannot be described, spoken to, or heard from.
- ❖ God is simply a strange fruit of strange imagination. God has no beginning or an end.
- ❖ God may be a discovery, an invention, a fanciful fictional imagination but is a peculiar source of entertainment, a wall to lean against.
- ❖ The believers in God are more relaxed. Their disposable time and money are less destructive.
- ❖ At least a third of humanity has been on murderous rampage for about two millennia as a commandment from the messenger of their God.

Lifeology and Curiosity

Lifeology and Curiosity

Astrology furnishes a magnificent proof of this miserable subjective tendency in men...The aim of astrology is to bring the motions of the celestial bodies into relation with the wretched Ego and to establish a connection between a comet in the sky and squabbles and atrocities on earth.
—*Arthur Schopenhauer*

Only a life lived for others is worth living-
—*Albert Einstein*

Lifeology and Curiosity

He who can no longer pause to wonder is as good as dead..... The eternal mystery of the world is its comprehensibility ... The fact that it is comprehensible is a miracle... "Man is, at one and the same time, a solitary being and a social being...."
—Albert Einstein

On the billions of years long time-line of the universe, the life-time of man is only a microscopic tiny speck; yet no living man ever grasps the fated fact that in a very short time he must return to wherever he came from. The living man witnesses sufferings and deaths of his fellow beings every day, and still keeps on living imprudently. He normally thinks and plans of the very short future that lies ahead of him, and thus lives off his whole life mostly by the day and day very stressfully. The most important quality of mind, specifically, inquisitiveness, is very early nipped in the bud by his inherited culture and totalitarian schooling. Man, in every corner of the globe, all through the history, has been busy trying get ahead of his neighbors, by oppressing, subjugating and massacring them. The oppressed have been fighting off oppressors without intervals as revealed by the entire documented history. Over millennia, thousands of philosophers, psychologists, epistemologists, metaphysicians, inventors of zillions of gods and goddesses, prophets and their followers have penned millions of pages, travelled far and wide to spread wisdom, compassion, humility, moderation, hatred and love to manipulate and control successfully and dreadfully lives of millions of people all over the world.

Lifeology is about intangible elements of human life that make life worth living. What we cannot see, touch, hear, taste and physically feel, can make us more happy or miserable than all the tangible — touchable — possessions or lack thereof. Intangibility is claimed to be the cause of the following forty five among approximately three hundred psychiatric disorders for which twenty percent world populations is being addictively drugged by psychiatrists:

Acute stress, adjustment, anorexia nervosa, antisocial personality, avoidant personality, bereavement, borderline personality, conduct, conversion, dependent personality, depersonalization, developmental coordination, of written expression, dissociative fugue, dissociative identity, exhibitionism, expressive language, factitious, generalized anxiety, general adaptation syndrome, histrionic personality, hyperactivity, intermittent explosive, kleptomania, mathematics, obsessive-compulsive, obsessive-compulsive personality, oppositional defiant, pain, panic attacks, panic, perfectionism, pervasive developmental, reading, reactive attachment, seasonal affective, self injury, separation anxiety, sadism and masochism, shared psychotic and social anxiety.
Psychiatrists, legally licensed experts in the treatment of mental disorders, and millions of patients depending on all the chemicals invented by pharmaceutical

giants, compose a very interesting episode in the study of lifeology- how people conduct their lives and how their lives are manipulated.

An ocean of mysteries engulfs us right from the day one of our lives. If we are tutored brightly, we would enjoy a lifelong fun full of curiosities every moment of our breath. The pursuit and accumulation of wealth by good and evil means has been a perpetual occupation of man's entire life, from the very childhood until the beginning of senility. One of the great misfortunes in one's life is a fortune that descends down from one's patrimony, for such an unearned fortune is destructive, monotonous and runs out extravagantly. Is it not a matter of utmost curiosity that as life starts entering its final phases, man begins to wonder about the past that he lived through, about the relationships he had had with the people who led or misled him, about the great opportunities that he ignored and the way he abused his own body and soul?

What future holds in its enormity for anyone has been a perpetual curiosity. Man has devised many strange inventions to peep into his future. Astrology has been just one of those inventions, Astronomy and astrology are inseparable from each other even though the former is truly scientific and later a concoction. The curiosity to know the future has been a perpetual ingredient of man's history and civilization. This curiosity about what blessed fortunes or catastrophic misfortunes he may enjoy or suffer from all his life is perhaps programmed in his DNA. All kinds of entrepreneurs invented both complex and simplistic black arts, divinations, fortune-telling, horoscopy, occultisms, and voodooisms.

Egyptians, Babylonians, Mesopotamians, Samarians, Romans, Greeks, Arabs, Indians and people from all nooks and corners of the world all the times wondered about their providence. They had little defense against natural disasters, diseases, invaders, famines and venomous insects. They felt insecure and helpless against the ravages that the next day or next year could bestow upon them. They had a rational reason to look for fortune-tellers. Emperors and their subjects, rulers and the ruled, rich and poor, masters and slaves, superbly literate and seriously illiterate, believers and atheists, politicians and their constituents, and men from all walks of life now and then looked for someone who could predict their tomorrows.

> *"The important thing is not to stop questioning. Curiosity has its own reason for existing. One cannot help but be in awe when he contemplates the mysteries of eternity, of life, of the marvelous structure of reality. It is enough if one tries merely to comprehend a little of this mystery every day. Never lose a holy curiosity."* —Albert Einstein

Wondering why the sun rises and sets, why the moon encircles our earth, why the universe is exactly infinite, why water pours from heavens, why wind blows, why volcanoes erupt, why an apple falls down to the ground and not up, why a little seed turns into a gigantic tree, why children are close but not very close copies of their parents, why a magnetic compass locks in only one direction, why we are born and why we die, and all many more 'whys' are the foundation stones on which the visionaries stand and spread the fruit of their imaginations and hard work for the benefit of all.

Righteousness is realized a little from books and schools. Most of it comes from parental heritage. Some of us are hit by a stroke of fine luck that orients us into a lifelong right direction; the rest are only at the mercy of random luck that scatters us in all kinds of random and changing tracks throughout our lives. We are dispersed in the vastness of our earth with a big empty mental bag that readily becomes occupied with all kinds of good and bad, wrong and right, constructive and destructive information, ideas, beliefs, notions, fervors, and fanaticism. We have some simple facts of life, like love of music, that we never wonder about. An attention to this strange phenomenon is bewildering. Just like taste, music cannot be defined or explained, it can only be experienced. Music is a powerful source of emotions, relaxation, and revolt. Celebration of joy and sometimes expression of sadness are incomplete without it. It appears to be an essential component of the very existence of nature. Oceans, wind, rivers, falls, and lightning are all musical in different ways. All sounds and music are basically vibration of material objects; some combination of these vibrations is music to our ears and some combinations are annoying and painful noise.

Conclusively!
Lifeology and Curiosity

- ❖ It was anxiety not curiosity that invented black arts, divinations, astrology, fortune-telling and horoscopy.
- ❖ Curiosity is the mother of a lively life and all the sparkles it encompasses.
- ❖ Only solitary minds through their organized planning are the roots of affluence.
- ❖ The pursuit and accumulation of wealth by good and evil means has been a perpetual occupation of man's entire life.
- ❖ To a curious mind everything is a miracle, to a dull mind nothing is miracle.

The Oral Law of Oration

To go on with the life peacefully
To sound brilliant and radiant
Diligent, relevant and intelligent
Let your gestures be modest
You may be an expert evidently
It is persuasive if narrated gently
Whatever you want to convey plausibly
It is true and honest
The law is omnipotent
Evident and persistent
That to SPEAK SOFTLY
Sweetly and smilingly
Is divine and saintly

Mathology and Curiosity

Mathology and Curiosity

Loosely translated:
With me, everything turns into
mathematics.....
More closely translated as:
but in my opinion,
all things in nature occur
mathematically.
—Rene' Descarte

Teaching and learning physics and math, of all scholastic disciplines, can be made so curiosity driven, entertaining and easy that students shall flock to study these subjects; it is possible only if the instructors are in love with physics and math and have very profound demonstrable comprehension of many real life applications of the laws of nature. Proficiency in physics and math grants a joy-ride to self-learn all other subjects.

Mathology and Curiosity

Pure mathematics is, in its way, the poetry of logical ideas.... "The creative principle [of science] resides in mathematics."
— *Albert Einstein*

Mathology is intrinsic in every nook and corner of the universe; it also drives our daily lives. Without it many scientific discoveries could have not been possible. It has thousands of applications and following four key classes:

- *Magnitude:* Measure of magnitude is the foundation of all mathology. Arithmetical counting in whole, fractions, decimals, infinitesimals to infinity, real or complex numbers represents magnitude. What we owe, own, when, and where, are the simplest examples of computation of magnitude.
- *Structure:* A mysterious quark, an atom, a molecule, a biological cell, a planet, a star, a whole galaxies, are a few examples of orderly mathological structures.
- *Space:* Comprehension and representation of space is not possible without the concept of lines, surfaces, and inclination between lines and surfaces. For this we needed plane, analytic, differential and algebraic geometry, plane and spherical trigonometry.

❖ *Change:* Change is perpetual because *time, the vehicle of change*, never rests or stops. Time is the most mysterious miracle of the universe, all changes occur in the realm of time. Forces, locations, temperatures, electromagnetic fields vary every instant. Differential and integral calculus is needed to analyze and study all changes.

This is the only segment of human knowledge that can be called precise, unambiguous, and perpetually true. This knowledge has to be given most of the credit for the technical progress we have made. Observations of the natural phenomena could have not been, linked, analyzed, and made to provide us with the conclusions that revealed to us the secrets of nature that are not observable with any combination of our sensory perceptions. Einstein wondered how could it be that mathematics — being, after all, a product of human thought, independent of experience — is so admirably adapted to the objects of reality? And Mach observed, strange as it may sound, the power of mathematics rests on its evasion of all unnecessary thought and its wonderful saving of mental maneuvers. Operation of Mother Nature is very simply a deep connection amongst distance, time, and mass, the most fundamental elements that can describe all natural phenomena in various numerical forms. For example, any kind of motion, force and energy is relative change in distance, time and mass. When we watch a TV or computer monitor screen, we are looking at a lot of very intricate math in action. Math is also the first foundation of every house, bridge, flying machine, skyscraper, ocean liner, moon rocket, fine musical instrument, computer, light bulb, atomic bomb, armored tank, textile designs, medical diagnostic and surgical instruments.

Next to math, physics indisputably is the least impure mathematically formulated set of the laws of nature derived from an immense amount of precise data collected by men and women of great perseverance, concentration, and diligence. Newton was perhaps the only genius who created completely new and powerful mathematical operations to analyze his own ideas relating physically observed data and thence to express the laws of nature in the most concise and precise mathematical relationships. The intuitive genius of Maxwell applied mathematical resources to translate all the knowledge on electricity and magnetism preceding him into very precise equations known as Maxwell's equations. Speed and many other inherent characteristics of light were deduced from these equations. Many important concepts in physics, which were later found to be true, were mathematical deductions.

Math and physics are prerequisites for all strictly clean and precise logical thinking. Study of these subjects teaches how to write and express clearly. The lack of training in these two vital subjects is the reason why sociologists, psychologists, philosophers, lawyers, and, most miserably politicians cannot express or write any idea concisely. They believe that a very large number of words and pages would convince or fool their audience or readers of any baseless, irrelevant and false information, in other words, if they give it a lot of mass, time, and length. Next, the two most important subjects, chemistry and molecular biology, are easy for us to comprehend on the foundation of math and physics. Thereafter, the rest of knowledge and information is more or less human-generated rules, procedures, stories, incidents, prejudices, imaginations, and their varied combinations, which requires only a dedicated memory machine to remember.

We can clearly see that whatever we call progress is the outcome of the knowledge we accumulated in math, physics, chemistry, and biology. All engineering, technology, drugs, medical procedures and diagnostics, space travel, internet explosion, entertainment wonders, and so on are the grandchildren of mathematicians, physicists, chemists, and biologists.

Zero and its position in decimal counting system is the most ingenious invention in mathology. No wonder, zero is represented by a circle or ellipse; it could have been symbolized by some other shape just as 1 thru 9 were. Perhaps the rotundity of sun, moon and planets was inspirational in the triumph upon a symbol for zero. Counting from 1 through 10 and then from 10

Mathology and Curiosity

to 100 and so on made arithmetical computation very easy and logical. The origin of the decimal counting or numbering system, 1 thru 9 and then 10 is credited to an Indian scholar named Aryabhata in about 500 AD.

It is India that gave us the ingenious method of expressing all numbers by means of ten symbols, each symbol receiving a value of position as well as an absolute value; a profound and important idea which appears so simple to us now that we ignore its true merit. But its very simplicity and the great ease which it has lent to computations put our arithmetic in the first rank of useful inventions; and we shall appreciate the grandeur of the achievement the more when we remember that it escaped the genius of Archimedes and Apollonius, two of the greatest men produced by antiquity.

— *Pierre-Simon Laplace*

It is difficult to comprehend if any counting system lacking the concept of zero is possible. Why and how zero took birth in India has some link with ancient Indian astronomy and astrology. Indian Hindus have deep faith in Brahmin astrologers' talent for predicting fortunes and futures. The relative locations of planets and moon at the time and location of one's birth required a degree of mathematical knowledge for astrological predictions .

As civilization progressed, one of the many curiosities was how to count material objects, and then possibly, how to sense and measure time, and finally how to weigh objects. On the time scale of thousands of years, the concept of measuring electric charge, energy, relative change and heat (or temperature) emerged only recently. Obviously, a simple counting system could not suffice the needs of measuring relative change, heat and energy.

Only on the foundation of decimal counting system, algebra, geometry, trigonometry and calculus took birth. Calculus is the greatest mathematical innovation next to the decimal counting system. All phenomena of nature, that obviously include all those of our lives, vary every moment. Without calculus to calculate such variations would be incomprehensible. Volumes and surface areas of all curved bodies cannot be calculated without calculus. All segments of science, technology, medicine, medical diagnostics, radioactive therapy, drug discovery and elimination, astronomy, economics, computer software, need calculus for optimal analysis. Maxwell's theory of electromagnetism and Einstein's theory of relativity are stated in differential calculus. All chemical reactions and radioactive decays need calculus for necessary conclusions. Curvilinear motion of smallest particles on our planet earth to gigantic celestial bodies can only be analyzed with the help of calculus. Isaac Newton discovered Laws of Motion and then created calculus for analyzing those Laws. Gottfried Leibniz is also credited for creating calculus independently.

Mathology and Curiosity

What did some eminent geniuses think of mathematics! To Galileo it was "The universe cannot be read until we have learned the language and become familiar with the characters in which it is written. It is written in mathematical language, and the letters are triangles, circles and other geometrical figures, without which it is humanly impossible to comprehend a single word." To Gauss it was "the Queen of the Sciences". To Hilbert it was " Mathematics is not like a game whose tasks are determined by arbitrarily stipulated rules. Rather, it is a conceptual system possessing internal necessity that can only be so and by no means otherwise." To Einstein it was "as far as the laws of mathematics refer to reality, they are not certain; and as far as they are certain, they do not refer to reality." Mathematics and all the laws of nature, completely expressible only in mathematical relationships, are indispensable tools to define, analyze and solve all puzzles of any description.

The following four most important laws of the universe are expressed in very precise and concise mathematical equations.

- ❖ Newton's universal law of gravitation-equations, the equations that can calculate what a mechanical system will do at any moment after it is set into motion
- ❖ Maxwell's equations that express relationship between electric and magnetic fields. These equations hide, hold and most precisely convey the secrets of the most imperceptible phenomena

of nature.
- ❖ Schrödinger's equation that describes the wave function of a quantum system comprising atomic and subatomic particles
- ❖ Einstein's energy equals mass times the speed of light squared, probably the most famous equation in history, completely changed our view of matter and reality; it led to nuclear fission power stations and nuclear (atomic) bombs. His theory of relativity made global positioning system possible by accounting for shrinking and expanding of time; if this change was not accounted for, our directions would be off by thousands of yards.

Mathematics, rightly viewed, possesses not only truth, but supreme beauty — a beauty cold and austere, like that of sculpture, without appeal to any part of our weaker nature, without the gorgeous trappings of painting or music, yet sublimely pure, and capable of a stern perfection such as only the greatest art can show. The true spirit of delight, the exaltation, the sense of being more than Man, which is the touchstone of the highest excellence, is to be found in mathematics as surely as poetry.
— *Bertrand Russell*

Amazingly music too, without which life will be very monotonous, is deeply related to mathematical analysis, creation, reproduction and electronic storage. Like all natural phenomena, sound has mathematical nature; music is entertaining and relaxing sound in many integrated frequencies. Electronic devices can mathematically produce sound of any past, present and future musical instrument, from a very low frequency vibrating drum or a very high frequency violin. Ancients of many lands, Chinese, Egyptians, Indians, Greeks and Mesopotamians investigated and analyzed mathematical nature of ordinary sound and musical sound. They realized, that very mysteriously, musical sound resulted in mental peace.

Form the very first to the last day of our lives money matters. And all money-matters are entrench in math, relatively not very sophisticated math. Our pay-checks, bank-transactions, buying and selling trades, legal contracts, stock-market ventures, IRS-autocracy, mortgages, insurance, legal, technical and medical services, entertainment, government and personal security, communications, all utilities, transportation, etc., are a few examples of how money-math rules our daily life.

There is nothing, absolutely nothing, no tangible comfort, entertainment, transport, housing, defense, communication, schooling, safe storage, climate control, political manipulations, voting predictions, weather-prediction, power generation, computation, water distribution, sewage disposal, today that does not relax on the power of mathematics.

For the health of the moral life, for ennobling

the tone of an age or a nation, the austerer virtues have a strange power, exceeding the power of those not informed and purified by thought. Of these austerer virtues the love of truth is the chief, and in mathematics, more than elsewhere, the love of truth may find encouragement for waning faith. Every great study is not only an end in itself, but also a means of creating and sustaining a lofty habit of mind; and this purpose should be kept always in view throughout the teaching and learning of mathematics.

— *Bertrand Russel*

Conclusively!
Mathology and Curiosity

- ❖ All elements of mathematics are flowers of the plant called curiosity.
- ❖ Pure mathematics is the poetry of logical ideas.
- ❖ Without mathematics the laws of the universe would still be mysteries.
- ❖ Precision and real productive intelligence is not viable without mathematics.
- ❖ Any information inexpressible mathematically is NOT trustworthy.

Prosperity and Curiosity

*Elementary History
of
Curiosity, Prosperity and Poverty*

Curiosity, prosperity and poverty are interlinked culturally, religiously and politically. Over the last half a millennium, 95% of all vital inventions and discoveries, seeded by curiosity, bloomed in West Europe and North America that made up only 5% of the humanity. Rest 95% of the humanity was engaged as: Chinese in imperial dynasties, Indians in inventing and housing thousands of gods, Middle Easterners in massacring nonbelievers, Africans and Australians in tribal dances, and Russians in Monarchism and Tsarism. Inventions and discoveries created prosperity only where ruling-elite was sane. Poverty perishes when insane politicians perish and freedom to succeed and fail is fully free.

Prosperity and Curiosity

All prosperity, without any exception, evolved and shall continue to evolve only due to the discovery and applications of the laws of nature.

Johannes Kepler, an astronomer and mathematician, discovered the laws of planetary motion and proved that the planets described elliptical paths around the sun. Galileo Galilei, a physicist and mathematician, built the most powerful telescope of his era that discovered many secrets of the solar system. He also explained why the states of constant velocity and absolute rest were indistinguishable. He showed that all free falling objects accelerated at the same rate. René Descartes, a philosopher, mathematician and physicist, envisioned the infiniteness of the universe and believed that all space was mysteriously occupied.

Isaac Newton, truly acclaimed to be the most ingenious mathematician and physicist of all times, discovered the laws of motion that reign the whole universe. He theorized that light was composed of particles. He invented the mathematical tool called calculus that he used to explore the omnipresence of the laws of motion and planetary motions.

Prosperity and Curiosity

Thomas Young, a physicist, for the first time exhibited with a double-slit experiment, that light had characteristics of waves. John Dalton, a chemist, theorized that each one of all elements was composed of indestructible and uniquely structured particles; such particles combined to build matter of every shape and characteristic. Michael Faraday, a scientist, proved that the motion of magnets and electricity were interrelated and that light too was related to electromagnetism. Can 'LIFE' emanate spontaneously from pure inorganic matter? The scientist Louis Pasteur experimentally proved that the answer was 'NO'. There is an impenetrable wall between living and non-living matter.

The physicist, James Clerk Maxwell, a genius of the ranks of Isaac Newton and Albert Einstein, mathematically and most ingeniously summarized all laws of electromagnetism in four concise equations. These equations hold many mysterious secrets of the universe, and are the foundation of many technological inventions and discoveries.

Physicist Henri Becquerel discovered radioactivity that meant that some elements were emitting elementary particles and/or high frequency electromagnetic waves. Physicist J. J. Thomson in a very unique experiment discovered the atomic particle called the electron. Physicist Max Planck gave birth to quantum mechanics, also known as quantum physics; that meant that energy in any form can exist only in multiples of a certain discrete value or quantum.

Albert Einstein, a superb genius of millennia, discovered and explained many secrets of the universe. The most celebrated is his equation about interchangeability of mass and energy. His Theory of Relativity very clearly shows that all uniform motion is relative and 'state of rest' has no existence. In his General Theory of Relativity, that unified special relativity and Newton's Law of Universal Gravitation, Einstein explained that gravity resulted from curvature of four-dimensional space-time. All heavenly objects were perpetually in a free falling mode and were describing shortest curved paths. He proved that the speed of light is same for all observers irrespective of their own speed of motion. He analyzed photoelectric effect and concluded that light behaved both as particles and waves; the light particles knows as photons ejected electron form certain materials under certain conditions and converted into electrical energy. His prediction that the gravitational force can bend light was naturally proved to be true. Supposedly his greatest blunder by his own belief, the 'cosmological constant' of the infinite universe has lately proved to be not far from a realty.

The mathematician Hermann Minkowski explained that Einstein's Theory of Relativity can only be comprehended in a four-dimensional space, the fourth dimension being 'Time'. in which existence and structure of space is a function of time. Chemist Ernest Rutherford conceived that atoms had planetary structures where electrons were encircling nucleus like planets around the sun.

The physicist Ernest Rutherford succeeded in converting, scientifically termed transmuting, nitrogen into oxygen by bombarding alpha particles into nitrogen. This process is truly man-made nuclear reaction. Biochemist Alexander Oparin theorized that some four billion years ago, a very random mixture of inorganic compounds including atmospheric gases combined to form very elementary organic compounds that perhaps gave rise to what may be termed 'life'. Mathematician and cosmologist Alexander Friedmann concluded form Einstein's general relativity field equations that the universe goes through expansion and contraction cycle through a time-period of hundreds of billions of years. Physicist Erwin Schrödinger discovered one of the most fundamental and revolutionary quantum-physics relationships in a very concise mathematical form. This relationship is known as Schrödinger wave equation. The physicist Paul Dirac advanced a partially convincing proof that the universe is made of matter and antimatter. How to create antimatter is still a mystery.

James Chadwick unearthed the neutron; and Carl Anderson the positron, a theoretical anti-electron particle. and the physicists John Cockcroft and Ernest Walton transmuted lithium into helium and some other elements using high energy protons,, This transmutation is known as "splitting the atom".

Prosperity and Curiosity

Astronomers Fritz Zwicky and Walter Baade rightly theorized that normal stars decayed into neutron stars that emitted cosmic rays. Zwicky also predicted the existence of mysterious dark matter. Astronomers Robert Wilson and Arno Penzias measured cosmic microwave background radiation, that has been a possible evidence of Big Bank theory of the origin of the universe.

Scanning Tunnelling Microscope, an invention by Gerd Binnig and Heinrich Rohrer, made it possible to visually see that matter is structured by spherical atoms aligned and stacked in an very orderly fashion. The idea of Special Relativity occurred to Einstein while riding a street car and looking at a clock tower; he envisioned that the passage of time is related to the relative motion of the observer. This relativity applies to the whole universe. In the beginning electric power used only direct current (DC); most of the work was done by Thomas Edison. Direct current motors are expensive to build and have to used brushes. Nikola Tesla came with the idea of Alternating current that could create rotating magnetic field and the transmission voltage could be stepped up are down . AC has transmission and use of electric power very efficient and economical.

The basics of how television could work came from the simple back-and-forth motion of a agricultural till. The inventor imagined that an electron beam could scan and reproduce an image by integrating back and forth motion of an electron beam. René Descartes was a physicist , mathematician, philosopher and devout religious man. He established a system to specify space and location of any time in that space, called Cartesian coordinate system —Analytical geometry and its links with algebra helped the discovery of infinitesimal calculus. A candy bar softened from inside near the electromagnetic field of a military radar. Percy Spencer, the radar engineer, concluded that the radar -field started heating the interior of the bar. This discovery turned into the invention of microwave oven.

Conclusively!
Prosperity and Curiosity

- ❖ Curious self-interest is the foundation of prosperity.
- ❖ Inherited prosperity ensures poverty.
- ❖ Lawful greed is necessary for prosperity.
- ❖ Obsession has forever led prosperity.
- ❖ Autocrats choke prosperity for they lack curiosity.
- ❖ Poverty and slavery are two rooms of the same penitentiary.

Tranquility and Curiosity

*"Satisfaction of one's curiosity is one of
the greatest sources of happiness in life."
~Dr. Linus Pauling*

Tranquility and Curiosity

The main task of the spirit is to free man from his ego... The great moral teachers of humanity were, in a way, artistic geniuses in the art of living
—Albert Einstein

One of the greatest inventions American ingenuity has made is the peace-pill, also known as tranquility-tablet. Why and how has American prosperity invaded upon American tranquility? Over one quarter population of America depends on tranquilizers for tranquility. About sixty years ago, Miltown, the first tranquility (peace of mind) pill was prescribed 36 million times. Now Americans have a over 100 different tranquilizing chemicals that help them attain to drugs-induced-tranquility.

All through documented history, in every religion, philosophy, theology, psychotherapy, psychiatric treatment, loving relationship, friendship, and so on, tranquility has been the primary objective. Consequently, tranquility picked up many synonyms; it means calmness, coolness, equanimity, serenity, stillness, composure, hush, imperturbability, order, peacefulness, placidity, quietness, quietude, repose, and rest.

Over 300 mental disorders invented, discovered,

Tranquility and Curiosity

classified and labeled by psychiatrists and psychotherapists are all possible synonyms of stressful states of mind. All such states are due to lack of mental tranquility, peace, serenity and calmness. A variety of drugless techniques have been conceived and are being practiced to put the mind in relaxation mode. Meditation is one of those techniques. Concentrating and directing the biological thinking process to slow down, to aim at only stress-less emotions like forgiveness, love, compassion, truthfulness and creativity may be termed "Meditation". Religious and spiritual sages have come up with an advanced from of meditation called Transcendental Meditation - that involves spiritual introspection, whatever that means - claimed to curb blood pressure, anxiety and depression.

Einstein theorized, and it was experimentally confirmed that relatively time can stretch and shrink, or clocks run faster or slower, due to gravitation, acceleration and velocity. Time, an indefinable entity, has similar stretching and shrinking characteristic in our lives. While deeply asleep time passes at infinite speed. While suffering from tooth-ache, ear-ache, or severe back-ache, time virtually stops. In highly stressed mental condition one is not sure if clock is running backward or forward; this is the situation when a man thinks of going back to God. Tranquility is deeply intertwined with the speed at which time not a clock moves. All earthly clocks run at exactly the same speed; but time for each one of us moves

Tranquility and Curiosity

at different speed; this speed is a correct measure of tranquility.

> *Scientists have long delved into time*
> *For its nature is truly sublime*
> *Its history may be brief or long*
> *But its supremacy is forever strong*
> *Philosophizing on time is hilarious*
> *For it is the ultimate mystery of cosmos*
> *No phenomenon as direction of time*
> *Is comprehensible or explainable*
> *Far more than God, the Almighty*
> *The origin and cause of time is*
> *More strange and glorious*
> *More elusive and multifarious*

Misplaced tranquility translates into many havocs; one of them is suicide. Globally close to one million people kill themselves due to financial hardships, poor interpersonal relationships, loneliness, mental disorders, professional failures, drugs abuse, long sickness, lingering physical pain, political torture, fanatic martyrdom, and social boycott. Economic levels do not have much relationship with self-destruction; statistically Americas, India, China, Australia, and Western Europe are on the same footing. Bizarrely, the likelihood of physicians committing suicide is about double that of non-physicians; physicians too are victims of alcohol and hard drugs; if they cannot project the kind of intellectual prowess and superior knowledge expected of them, they suffer from eccentric depression, and tend to destroy themselves.

We have bases within and without us that determine the peace we enjoy or the turmoil we suffer from. The familial, religious, cultural, and social environment we were raised in forms the frame of our minds for our inner peace. The politicians of our own and neighboring countries decide how much peace they will let us live in and with; historically, politicians and peace have rarely coexisted. Of the two sides of human nature, the ghastly side is far bigger than the pleasant side.

Nature has gifted us with fight or flight instinct for survival, so we do not know, when and how the concept of peace came about and to which ancient civilization the origin of this concept should be credited. We do know that the power hungry, the invaders, the warriors, and the wantons do not and did not dream of it. Peace is all these ingredient compounded: tranquility, serenity, freedom from anxiety, feeling of security, lack of mental agitation, selfless and harmless attachment with something or someone, and above all, hatred for none.

Past never was, future never shall be
Whatever happens, is in the present
Whatever would happen tomorrow
Shall happen when tomorrow is today
What is reality and what illusion

Tranquility and Curiosity

Is the question no one can rejoin
From east, west, north and south
And all nooks of the earth
For many millennium
Saints, philosophers and scientists
Have failed to break the mystery of mind
The true path to freedom
And seeds of wisdom
Lounge in laughter and smile
To make life purely tranquille

Our lives roll on a set of three mismatched wheels right from the first day of our birth. Fortune, fate and luck are these wheels. Fortune locks in at the moment of birth; fate is the environment that an individual can hardly change; luck is the random unprejudiced stroke that ruins or rewards poor and rich, week and strong without any discrimination. Present is infinitesimally short, past and future infinitely long. The past cannot be altered, and the future is unknown. The past cannot be lived in, but it is our constant companion, as we see, it very significantly determines what may our future be.

Tranquility is about choosing, curiosity over anxiety, serenity over ferocity, compassion over cruelty, liberty over slavery, vigor over lethargy, innovation over imitation, humility over pride, generosity over greed, love over hatred, knowledge over ignorance, and courage over cowardice.

Conclusively!
Tranquility and Curiosity

- ❖ Tranquility and happiness have to coexist.
- ❖ Tranquility is unrelated to fame and fortune.
- ❖ Tranquility is not viable without curiosity.
- ❖ Nature Deficiency Disorder chokes both curiosity and tranquility.
- ❖ Sooner or later
  One way or the other
  You shall be on for departure
  Despite, you came from wherever
  So, be humble, never brash
  For you can perish in a flash
  Don't be arrogant and vile
  While you are free and alive
  Live and let others live
  Smile and let others smile

Simplicity and Curiosity

Simplicity and Curiosity

God always takes the simplest way... I believe that a simple and unassuming manner of life is best for everyone, best both for the body and the mind.
— *Albert Einstein*

Simplicity and Curiosity

"If you can't explain it to a six year old, you don't understand it yourself — Possessions, outward success, publicity, luxury - to me these have always been contemptible. I believe that a simple and unassuming manner of life is best for everyone, best for both the body and the mind."
— *Albert Einstein*

Truth is ever to be found in the simplicity, and not in the multiplicity and confusion of things... Nature is pleased with simplicity. And nature is no dummy"
— *Isaac Newton*

It is very interesting and astonishing that the words 'simplicity and curiosity' are not found anywhere in millions of pages of texts and indexes of almost all famous books authored by famous professors of famous schools on variety of subjects that try to perk up lives of all kinds of people all over the world. These words are absent from works that deeply concentrate on subject-matters about business, computing, divinity, economics, management, philosophy, political science, psychology, self-improvement, sociology and religion. All these learned professors had no use of 'simplicity' in their thinking, analysis and description of their ideas and observations. No best sellers, both fiction and nonfiction, running into innumerable pages, dealing with human emotions had also nothing to do with simplicity.

All schooling, knowledge, professions, interests, pastimes and hobbies can be strictly positioned on only two paths; first is scientific and second unscientific. Simplicity and curiosity, it appears, goes only with and on scientific paths. Does scientific thinking leads to simplicity! All great scientists agree that the answer is yes. Unscientific knowledge is seat-of-the-pants expertise and cannot have any relationship with simplicity. The brains of unscientific 'experts' do not have any space to house simplicity and curiosity.

Science is defined as an organized knowledge about the laws of nature comprising the entire universe. All scientific relationships represent the laws of nature derived from the best fit that a large set of empirical data can provide. Very strangely, most of the laws of nature are concise and are relationships involving only few parameters and entities; this fact indicates that laws of nature are simple, and simplicity is the essence of nature. Aristotle, Galileo, Newton, Einstein and many other eminent scientists believed that the laws of the universe were comprehensible and simple. Newton emphasized that nature did not indulge in the lavishness of unnecessary causes. Some theologians claim that it is God's compassion and generosity that

Simplicity and Curiosity

His universe is simple and comprehensible.

Simplicity is indefinable for it is as much an abstract concept as beauty, sympathy and friendship, etc. And also, although simplicity is immeasurable, it has an acceptable valuation in all real life affairs. How we attire, buy, cook, earn, eat, educate, explain, learn, lecture, manage, pray, sell, spend and teach can be done in very easy or difficult way, or with simplicity or complexity.

Concision is the most important essence of all laws of nature; God appears to love it. The innermost secrets of the universe need mere one-line statements. The more we need to describe an idea, the less accurate and more confusing it becomes. Simplicity strikes like lightning. A microscopic cell contains more intelligence and information than a whole life form. An atom holds more energy internally than a million atoms externally. Nothing empowers rhetoric and humor more than brevity.

Simplicity may be as much of a conceptual emotion as many other emotions like annoyance, ecstasy, euphoria, happiness, hysteria, love, lust, satisfaction, self-confidence, etc. Simplicity does appear to have some bond with easiness and clarity. When man was emerging from the very natural primitive survival hardships some thousands of years ago, he sought mental and physical relaxation. Some discoveries and inventions made daily chores easier and faster. The

Simplicity and Curiosity

wheel, an intuitive derivative of the rotundity of sun, moon and tree trunks, definitely made moving large objects simple. and Some inventions, particularly pertaining to gods and goddesses took away immense amount of simplicity from man's life.

> *"Nature does not multiply things unnecessarily;*
> *that she makes use of the easiest and simplest means for producing her effects;*
> *that she does nothing in vain, and the like."*
> — *Galileo Galilei*

> *The grand aim of all science…is to cover the greatest possible number of empirical facts by logical deductions from the smallest possible number of hypotheses or axioms.*
> — *Albert Einstein*

Most of the Nobel laureates in physics, chemistry and medicine believed that simplicity-structured their thinking to a very great extent. They sharpened their curiosity to define it very precisely. Simplicity does not carry the same meaning for a mathematician, a physicist, an economist, an entertainer, an autocrat, a marketer, a philosopher, a beauty-contester, a superb chef, and a jeweler. So simplicity at best is a very fuzzy concept with many rationalizations. Leibniz hypnotized that the light-rays taking the shorted path

Simplicity and Curiosity

to travel from here to there is an important sign of simplicity in nature. Kepler, Newton and Maxwell were not far from such a belief. Metaphysically and theologically, God has created the universe very simplistically.

Common youth has never sought and does not seek simplicity. Unless specifically philosophized for a simple life, the youth like a south or north pole is ceaselessly seeking the opposite pole, male for a female and female for a male. Simplicity is only a meaningless and theoretical concept to common man. Heaving teens usually exhibit themselves as if they just emerged from a heap of garbage, or from an expensive beauty salon, or too bored after completing a monotonous work-day. For them the idea of a simple life or simplicity is bizarre; life is meaningless if one is worried about getting meaning out of it.

Only geniuses do and practice simplicity in their work and life. Here by geniuses we should only mean mathematicians and physicists. Scholars drenched in liberal arts cannot impart their thoughts in at least ten times the words truly needed to clarify their intellectuality; they cannot simplify anything.

Common man, irrespective of his financial worth, or era of history, abhors simplicity. All his life he seeks more and more of all that he catches sight of , pours and pushes down his esophagus all that is palatable. Autocrats, bureaucrats, politicians, and their cronies

Simplicity and Curiosity

not only abhor simplicity, they love complexity and convolutions, for that is the lifestyle that they want to live and die for.

The quality of being simple, plain, peaceful, truthful and honest, free from complexity, is not locked in pretentiousness and hypocrisy. Simplicity and curiosity have always coexisted, and shall ever coexist. Inherited prosperity is toxic to a simple life. It is well established that any inherited fortune is a misfortune. Ultimately, any venture that doesn't have a leader who believes in simplicity will soon die. The secret is, to survive, stay simple.

> *"The ingenious method of expressing all numbers by means of ten symbols, each symbol receiving a value of position as well as an absolute value; a profound and important idea which is so simple to us now that we ignore its true merit. But its very simplicity and the great ease which it has lent to computations put our arithmetic in the first rank of useful inventions."*
> *— Pierre-Simon Laplace*

The concept of simplicity also gave birth to irreplaceable metaphysical Divine Simplicity Doctrine that describes God and all the attributes of God. For God lacks all tangible compositions, God is nature and nature is God, all attributes of

Simplicity and Curiosity

God are completely identical. God is omniscient and omniscience is God. Essentially, Divine Simplicity Doctrine is as complex as simple and only God alone can explain what is simple and not complex about God.

Historically, all over the world, from one corner to the other, people have worked hard to complicate their lifestyles. Now all tasks and acts or speedier, more automated but by no means more enjoyable. How they earn a livelihood, how they transport their bodies or their goods, how they mutilate their food and food-stuff, how they start, maintain and ruin their human-relationships, how they stuff their bodies with dangerous delicatessens, all that is anti-simplified.

> *"That's been one of my mantras — focus and simplicity. Simple can be harder than complex: You have to work hard to get your thinking clean to make it simple. But it's worth it in the end because once you get there, you can move mountains."*
> *— Steve Jobs*

Conclusively!
Simplicity and Curiosity

- ❖ The first law of nature is Simplicity.
- ❖ Curiosity feeds off simplicity
- ❖ Only mathematical and scientific minds comprehend and practice simplicity.
- ❖ Poor and rich alike work hard to complicate their lives.
- ❖ Autocrats and bureaucrats, abhor simplicity and love complexity and convolutions.

Curiosity Postlude

*Only ceaseless curiosity
can fashion the future
for freedom, fortune and
fortitude.*

Postlude

Curiosity and job-security enjoy perpetual hostility toward each other.

- ❖ Mark Twain, an ardent observer of human nature, truly believed "There is no distinctly native American Criminal class except Congress...All Congresses and Parliaments have a kindly feeling for idiots, and a compassion for them, on account of personal experience and heredity." Sadly, the vocabulary of this class does not include the word *curiosity* in any form or shape.
- ❖ Autocratic bureaucracy empowered by the American lawyers' oligarchy has been working hard to enslave American population for running to the government bureaucratic utopia to kill creative curiosity that made America the most prosperous land on the globe.
- ❖ The factual data, that percentage of self-employed American population shrank from 25% to only 4% in the last fifty years, confirms the peccadillo of the bureaucracy and demise of creativity.
- ❖ Unionization of any kind is an expression of collapse of curiosity among all members of the union. Teachers' union is no exception to this rule. Incurious teachers cannot bolster curiosity of young minds.
- ❖ It is futile to expect politically empowered teachers' unions, not to convert curious young minds into cogs of obedience to fit into shackle of boring repetitive jobs.

- ❖ *'Guaranteed job security'* of government bureaucrats and peons is synonym of incuriosity, apathy and lethargy.
- ❖ All math-less and science-less schooling should be labeled as edification not as education. Nature, wherein all the curiosity is contained, could have not been in the past and cannot be in the future explored without math and science.
- ❖ Schooling, teaching, education, and learning should be mainly about how to keep naturally instinctive curiosity active and vibrant in budding minds so that these minds could enjoy very creative lives.
- ❖ Intelligence of children is usually inadequately gauged and very poorly developed; it is because only mediocre people choose to go into teaching profession due to relatively very poor remunerative rewards.
- ❖ Children are immensely curious; they want to learn and discover and explore. Their curiosity is strangled and stifled by their parents, teachers, politicians and passive entertainments.
- ❖ All infants enter the world as bundles of joy and curiosity. At departure from their world most of them are bundles of anxiety, grief and depression for they live incurious and monotonous lives.
- ❖ Depression is normally the result of boredom, lethargy, dependency, alcoholism and loneliness; but psychiatrists have addicted 20% of the world population on host of dangerous anti-depressants that strangle natural human curiosity and creativity.